ELECTION
PERSPECTIVES

A 30-DAY DEVOTIONAL ON HOW TO CAST YOUR VOTE
WHILE REMAINING "ONE" WITH THE BODY OF CHRIST

Terry M. Davis

Election Perspectives
Copyright © 2024 by Terry M. Davis

All rights reserved. No part of this book may be reproduced, distributed, or transmitted in any form or by any means, including photocopying, recording, or other electronic or mechanical methods, without the prior written permission of the author, except for brief quotations in a book review or scholarly article.

ISBN: 979-8-9892129-9-6

Self-Published by Terry M. Davis
Philadelphia, PA 19104

Printed in the United States of America

Scripture quotations are from the Holy Bible, New International Version® (NIV®).
Copyright © 1973, 1978, 1984, 2011 by Biblica, Inc.®
Used by permission. All rights reserved worldwide.

For permission requests, email the author at
Info@philadelphiagospelmovement.org or visit
https://www.philadelphiagospelmovement.org/

TABLE OF CONTENTS

Introduction 5

Day 1 | The Priority of Unity 7

Day 2 | Love Beyond Differences 9

Day 3 | Choosing Unity Over Division 11

Day 4 | The Power of Humility 13

Day 5 | The Ministry of Reconciliation 15

Day 6 | The CGA Fast 17

Day 7 | Bearing One Another's Burdens 19

Day 8 | The Bond of Peace 21

Day 9 | Building Bridges 23

Day 10 | A Higher Calling 25

Day 11 | The Unity of the Spirit 27

Day 12 | Our Common Mission 29

Day 13 | Be Quick to Listen, Slow to Speak 31

Day 14 | Humility in Disagreements 33

Day 15 | One Body, Many Parts 35

Day 16 | Choosing Love Over Fear 37

Day 17 | Let No Division Be Among You 39

Day 18 | Overcoming Evil with Good 41

Day 19 | Our True Citizenship 43

Day 20 | Praying for Our Leaders 45

Day 21 | The Call to Be Salt and Light 47

Day 22 | Guarding Our Hearts 49

Day 23 | The Power of Prayer 51

Day 24 | Trusting in God's Sovereignty 53

Day 25 | Kingdom Minded 55

Day 26 | Loving Our Enemies 57

Day 27 | Unity in Diversity 59

Day 28 | A Heart of Compassion 61

Day 29 | The Fruit of the Spirit 63

Day 30 | Keeping the Faith 65

Conclusion 67

INTRODUCTION

Voting is important. There have been many who have fought for our freedoms. One of the freedoms in our nation is the ability to vote for those who would become our elected officials on various levels. Within this nation, there are men and women running for Congress, the Senate, court justices, governors, mayors, and, most notably, for the President and Vice President of the United States. These offices are held by individuals often representing political parties. When we vote, we choose certain individuals, because they align with our values. Their policies often represent how we feel, and influence how this nation operates. To that end, it is important to cast your vote.

As Christians, our ultimate allegiance is to the kingdom of God, not just to earthly political systems. Yet, we also know that the kingdom of God uses men and women on this earth to fulfill His purposes and plans. This devotional will guide you through 30 days of scripture, reflection, and prayer, helping you navigate the complexities of voting, while maintaining unity within the Body of Christ. Most importantly, this devotion encourages you to seek God's heart and desire for His Kingdom to come, and His will to be done on earth as it is in heaven (Matthew 6:10). Remember, it's not only about who wins an election, but also about being intentional about living in a way that honors Jesus's prayer for advancing His kingdom and oneness in the Body of Christ.

Day 1 | The Priority of Unity

That all of them may be one, Father, just as you are in me and I am in you. May they also be in us so that the world may believe that you have sent me.
John 17:21 (NIV)

Jesus's prayer for unity reveals the deep desire of His heart for His followers to be one in Him. The oneness Jesus prayed for is not just agreement or politeness, but a profound spiritual unity that reflects the relationship He shares with the Father. This unity serves a greater purpose: it testifies to the world that Jesus was sent by the Father. In this election season, the world is watching how the Church responds to division. Will we allow political differences to fracture our relationships, or will we display the unity that Jesus prayed for? The way we engage with one another-especially when we disagree - speaks volumes about our faith. Unity in the Body of Christ is not a passive ideal but a powerful witness. As we navigate political choices, let us prioritize God's heart, as well as our spiritual unity, remembering that we all belong to Christ first, as well as to one another.

Prayer:
Father, I long for the unity that Jesus prayed for to be manifested in my life and in Your Church. Let me not be swayed by political agendas or disagreements, but remind me daily that I am part of something greater— a heavenly family united in Christ. Help me to lay down any pride, fear, or anger that keeps me from walking in unity with my brothers and sisters. Holy Spirit, soften my heart and increase my love for the Body of Christ, that I may pursue unity

with the same passion that Jesus displayed. May our oneness glorify You and be a testimony to the world of Your love and truth. In Jesus's name, amen.

Day 2 | Love Beyond Differences

A new command I give By this everyone will know that you are my disciples, if you love one another you: Love one another. As I have loved you, so you must love one another.
John 13: 34-35 (NIV)

Jesus calls us to love one another as He has loved us—unconditionally, sacrificially, and consistently. Political differences should never overshadow this command. The love that Jesus describes is not based on agreement or shared opinions but on His own selfless example and commitment to the Father. Loving someone who thinks differently than we do, especially in matters of politics, can be challenging. But, our love for one another is meant to be a distinguishing mark of our beliefs. When we love beyond differences, we reflect the heart of God, who loves each of us. During this election season, as tensions rise and opinions clash, let your love for your fellow believers shine. This love is not a passive feeling but an active choice— a decision to honor, respect, and serve one another despite disagreements. In doing so, we fulfill Jesus's command and show the world what it truly means to follow Him.

Prayer:
Lord Jesus, You have shown me what true love looks like through Your life, death, and resurrection. Teach me to love my brothers and sisters as You have loved me—with patience, grace, and humility. When political differences tempt me to withdraw or lash out, remind me of Your command to love above all else. I want my love for others to be so deep, so genuine, that it becomes a testimony of my faith in You. Holy Spirit, fill my heart with the love of

Christ faith in You. Holy Spirit, fill my heart with the love of Christ and help me to extend that love to those who are difficult to love. Let my love reflect the depth of Your love for me, that others may see You in me. In Your name, amen.

Day 3 | Choosing Unity Over Division

Make every effort to keep the unity of the Spirit through the bond of peace.
Ephesians 4:3 (NIV)

Unity requires intentional effort. Paul urges us to "make every effort" to maintain the unity of the Spirit, which means we must actively choose to preserve peace, even when it's hard. Division comes easily- especially in politics-but unity takes commitment, humility, and grace. This unity is not something we create; it is a gift of the Spirit, and our job is to preserve it. We do this through the bond of peace, choosing to pursue reconciliation over resentment and understanding over judgment. In the context of political disagreements, this may mean using wisdom, discernment, and grace in the conversations that God may lead us to have with fellow believers, but also letting go of the need to engage in unnecessarily divisive arguments. It means valuing relationships more than opinions and remembering that Christ, and our unity in Christ, is far more important than our political affiliations. This is not about uniformity of thought, but about inviting God's peace that comes from being one in Christ.

Prayer:
Father, I confess that it is sometimes easier to choose division than unity, especially when I feel strongly about certain political matters. But I know that You have called me to a higher way-to make every effort to keep the unity of the Spirit through peace. Help me to be a peacemaker in every situation, to seek understanding and reconciliation rather than winning arguments. Holy Spirit, give me the strength to preserve unity, even when it feels Holy Spirit, give

me the strength to preserve unity, even when it feels difficult or uncomfortable winning arguments. Holy Spirit, give me the strength to preserve unity, even when it feels Holy Spirit, give me the strength to preserve unity, even when it feels difficult or uncomfortable. Let my words and actions reflect the wisdom and peace of the Holy Spirit, so that I may honor you and contribute to the unity of Your Church. In Jesus's name, amen.

Day 4 | The Power of Humility

Do nothing out of selfish ambition or vain conceit. Rather, in humility value others above yourselves, not looking to your own interests but each of you to the interests of the others.
Philippians 2:3-4 (NIV)

Humility is the foundation of unity. Without it, division and pride quickly take root. Paul calls us to value others above ourselves and to consider their interests before our own. This is especially relevant during election seasons when political debates can easily become about proving who is right or wrong. But humility invites us to listen rather than argue, to seek to understand rather than to be understood. It calls us to recognize the worth of every person, regardless of their political views, and to honor them as image-bearers of God. Humility is not thinking less of yourself but thinking of yourself less, placing the needs and concerns of others before your own. As you navigate this election season, let humility guide your interactions with others. Choose to listen, learn, and love, even when it's hard.

Prayer:
Lord, humility does not always come naturally to me, especially when I feel strongly about my opinions. But I know that humility is the key to unity and peace in Your Church. Help me to walk in humility, considering the needs and interests of others above my own. Teach me to listen more than I speak, to understand rather than argue, and to love without condition. Holy Spirit, humble my heart and align it with the heart of Christ, who did not seek His own glory but gave Himself for others. Let this same attitude be in me, that I may contribute to the unity of Your Body. In Jesus's name, amen.

Day 5 | The Ministry of Reconciliation

All this is from God, who reconciled us to himself through Christ and gave us the ministry of reconciliation: that God was reconciling the world to himself in Christ, not counting people's sins against them. And he has committed to us the message of reconciliation.
2 Corinthians 5:18-19 (NIV)

As followers of Christ, we have been entrusted with the ministry of reconciliation. This goes beyond reconciling people to God—it also includes reconciling relationships with one another. Political differences can create rifts in families, churches, and friendships, but we are called to be agents of reconciliation, healing divisions, and bringing peace. Reconciliation requires humility, forgiveness, and love. It means not holding people's offenses against them, just as God does not hold our sins against us. In this season, seek opportunities to bring healing where there is division. Be a voice of reconciliation, offering grace instead of judgment and peace instead of conflict. Remember that we are all united in Christ, and our calling is to build bridges, not walls.

Prayer:
Father, thank You for reconciling me to Yourself through Christ. I ask for Your grace to extend that same reconciliation to others, especially in times of division and disagreement. Give me the courage to be a peacemaker, to seek out opportunities to heal broken relationships, and to bring unity where there is discord. Holy Spirit, fill my heart with Your love and forgiveness so that I may freely give it to others. Use me as an instrument of reconciliation in my family, my church, and my community, that Your kingdom may be revealed through our unity. In Jesus's name, amen.

Day 6 | The CGA Fast

Do not let any unwholesome talk come out of your mouths, but only what is helpful for building others up according to their needs, that it may benefit those who listen.
Ephesians 4:29 (NIV)

This verse from Paul's writing to the Church at Ephesus is a great reminder that words matter. If we're not careful we can develop the habit of using the wrong kinds of words when speaking to or about our Christian brothers and sisters. What if we fasted from words that harm, just as we would fast from food? That's the heart of the CGA Fast—an intentional break from Complaining, Gossip, and Accusation (CGA).

You are invited over the next 21 days to practice the CGA Fast and pursue greater unity in the Body of Christ. Just as fasting from food brings clarity and renewal to our spirits, fasting from Complaining, Gossip, and Accusation (CGA) allows our hearts and minds to align more fully with Heaven's culture of love and honor. This fast is not simply about abstaining from harmful words or attitudes; it's about creating space for God to work in us and through us to foster deeper unity among believers. Even when we disagree. With the Holy Spirit's help, we can replace negative habits with gratitude, honor, and love—building unity and reflecting the heart of Christ.

Prayer:
Lord, as I embark on this CGA fast, I ask for Your grace to help me refrain from complaining, gossiping, and accusing. Instead Lord, please let my words and thoughts reflect Your love, grace, and

encouragement. May I be an agent of that unity, speaking life and building up those around me. Please strengthen me by Your Spirit to walk in gratitude, honor, and love each day. In Jesus's name, amen.

Day 7 | Bearing One Another's Burdens

Carry each other's burdens, and in this way, you will fulfill the law of Christ.
Galatians 6:2 (NIV)

In a world increasingly marked by individualism, the call to bear one another's burdens feels countercultural, yet it is central to the life of a believer. This isn't just about helping others with physical or emotional needs—it's also about standing with them in times of spiritual, relational, or political strain. In times of political tension, our differences can feel heavy. We can be quick to distance ourselves from those whose perspectives challenge us. But Scripture calls us to bear those burdens together, to engage with love, patience, and understanding. To fulfill the law of Christ (Mark 12:30-31) – the law to love the Lord, our God, with all ourselves, and love our neighbor as ourselves – means walking alongside one another even in times of disagreement, providing support and care rather than criticism. By doing this, we imitate Christ, who bore our greatest burden: sin and separation from God. In the political sphere, this could mean listening without judgment, providing comfort rather than critique, and focusing on unity rather than differences.

Prayer:
Lord, I know that I cannot bear the weight of my own burdens, let alone those of others, without Your help. Thank You for carrying my burdens daily and for never growing weary. Teach me to bear the burdens of my brothers and sisters with the same love, patience, and grace that You show me. Open my eyes to the needs around me—especially the burdens that may be hidden beneath the surface. Help me to love deeply, even in the midst of

disagreements. Let my willingness to share the weight of others' burdens be a reflection of Your love and an act of worship to You. In Jesus's name, amen.

Day 8 | The Bond of Peace

And over all these virtues put on love, which binds them all together in perfect unity. Let the peace of Christ rule in your hearts, since as members of one body you were called to peace. And be thankful.
Colossians 3:14-15 (NIV)

Love is the glue that holds unity together. Paul reminds us that love binds all virtues—compassion, kindness, humility, and gentleness—into perfect unity. But he doesn't stop there; he calls us to let the peace of Christ rule in our hearts. When peace rules, it governs our thoughts, actions, and interactions with others. This peace isn't merely the absence of conflict; it's a deep, abiding sense of well-being and wholeness that comes from being rooted in Christ. Political seasons are often fraught with tension, but we are called to be peacemakers, allowing Christ's peace to flow through us into every conversation, relationship, and decision. Our unity as believers is not contingent on our agreement with each other but on our shared bond in Christ. When love and peace guide us, the Church can weather any storm of division, remaining united and strong in its witness to the world.

Prayer:
Father, thank You for the peace of Christ that surpasses all understanding. Let that peace rule in my heart, so that I may be a vessel of Your peace in my interactions with others. Help me to put on love above all else, binding together the virtues You desire in my life with the strength of Your love. May I be a peacemaker, not a peacekeeper, willing to engage in difficult conversations but

always seeking unity and understanding. Let the world see Your love in me and in the Body of Christ as we walk in peace together. In Jesus's name, amen.

Day 9 | Building Bridges

If it is possible, as far as it depends on you, live at peace with everyone.
Romans 12:18 (NIV)

The command to live at peace with everyone comes with a key phrase: "as far as it depends on you." This reminds us that while we cannot control the actions, thoughts, or beliefs of others, we are responsible for our own. Peace is not passive; it is an intentional pursuit. In politically charged environments, peace may seem elusive, especially when conversations become heated or divisive. But peace is not simply the avoidance of conflict-it is actively seeking reconciliation and understanding. When we live as peacemakers, we become bridge-builders, connecting people rather than dividing them. We must make the effort to engage in compassionate dialogue and to look for ways to share God's truth, while also bringing others together. As believers, we should be known for the bridges we create, ensuring that peace and unity are always within reach.

Prayer:
Lord, I desire to be a bridge-builder in a world that often seeks to divide. Help me to pursue peace in every situation, as far as it depends on me. Give me the wisdom to know when to speak and when to listen, and the humility to put others' needs above my own. Let my words and actions reflect Your peace and Your heart for unity. Teach me to be an agent of reconciliation in my family, my community, and my church. May Your peace reign in me, and through me, draw others into deeper relationship with You and with each other. In Jesus's name, amen.

Day 10 | A Higher Calling

But you are a chosen people, a royal priesthood, a holy nation, God's special possession, that you may declare the praises of him who called you out of darkness into his wonderful light.
1 Peter 2:9 (NIV)

As believers, we are called to something higher than earthly agendas or cultural divisions. We are a chosen people, a royal priesthood, and a holy nation. Our primary identity is not rooted in our nationality, political affiliation, or cultural background but in our status as God's special possession. This identity calls us to live differently—to rise above the divisions of the world and declare the praises of God, who has brought us into His wonderful light. This higher calling should shape how we engage with the world, particularly in times of political tension. We are ambassadors of Christ's kingdom, and our words and actions should reflect the values of that kingdom: truth, love, mercy, justice, and peace. When we focus on our heavenly calling, we can navigate political differences with grace, knowing that we are part of a greater story.

Prayer:
Father, thank You for calling me out of darkness and into Your marvelous light. Help me to live out my higher calling as Your chosen one, a member of Your royal priesthood. Let my life declare Your praises, even in the midst of political differences and cultural divisions. Remind me daily that my true identity is found in You, not in earthly affiliations or titles. Holy Spirit, guide my thoughts, words, and actions so that I reflect the values of Your kingdom. May I bring light into every conversation and situation, always pointing others to You. In Jesus's name, amen.

Day 11 | *The Unity of the Spirit*

There is one body and one Spirit, just as you were called to one hope when you were called; one Lord, one faith, one baptism; one God and Father of all, who is over all and through all and in all.
Ephesians 4:4-6 (NIV)

Unity is not an optional aspect of our faith; it is woven into the very fabric of who we are as the Body of Christ. Paul reminds us that we are united by one Spirit, one hope, one Lord, and one faith. This unity is not something we create—it is a gift from God, rooted in the reality that we are all members of the same body, under the same Lord. As such, we are called to live in a way that reflects this spiritual truth. In times of political division, it can be tempting to focus on what separates us rather than what unites us. But our unity in Christ is far more powerful and enduring than any earthly differences. We must intentionally focus on our shared identity as members of one body, refusing to let political affiliations or opinions fracture our fellowship.

Prayer:
Lord, thank You for the unity that You have given us through Your Spirit. Help me to walk in that unity, even when the world around me seems divided. Remind me that I am part of one body, with one hope, one faith, and one Lord. Let this truth guide my thoughts and actions, so that I may contribute to the unity of the Body of Christ. Holy Spirit, empower me to be a force for unity, bridging gaps and healing divisions in Your Church. Let my life be a testimony of the power of Your Spirit to unite us all. In Jesus's name, amen.

Day 12 | Our Common Mission

Therefore go and make disciples of all nations, baptizing them in the name of the Father and of the Son and of the Holy Spirit, and teaching them to obey everything I have commanded you. And surely I am with you always, to the very end of the age.
Matthew 28:19-20 (NIV)

The Great Commission is the ultimate mission of the Church, and it transcends all political and cultural boundaries. Our calling is to make disciples of all nations, to baptize them, and to teach them to obey Christ's commands. This mission is far greater than any political platform or party. It is a global, eternal calling that unites us as believers and gives us a common purpose. In the heat of political debates, it's easy to lose sight of this mission. But we must remember that our primary allegiance is to Christ and His kingdom, and our primary task is to spread the good news of His love and grace. When we focus on our common mission, we can rise above political differences and work together to advance God's kingdom on earth.

Prayer:
Father, thank You for entrusting me with the mission of making disciples. Help me to keep this mission at the forefront of my mind, especially in times of political tension. Remind me that my primary calling is to share the Gospel in love and to help others grow in their relationship with You. Let this mission unite me with my brothers and sisters, even when we disagree on certain matters. Holy Spirit, guide me as I seek to live out the Great Commission in my daily life. May my words and actions point others to You and bring glory to Your name. In Jesus's name, amen.

Day 13 | Be Quick to Listen, Slow to Speak

My dear brothers and sisters, take note of this: Everyone should be quick to listen, slow to speak, and slow to become angry.
James 1:19 (NIV)

In the heat of political conversations, emotions can easily get the best of us. We may feel the need to defend our views or challenge others, often speaking hastily. But James gives us a powerful reminder: be quick to listen and slow to speak. This is not just wise advice for maintaining harmony in societal matters, but it is also key to unity in the Body of Christ. When we truly listen—seeking to understand rather than to respond—we create space for empathy, grace, and mutual respect. Listening honors the image of God in others, acknowledging that their perspective matters, even if it differs from our own. Slow, thoughtful speech allows us to speak truth in love, without contributing to anger or division. In this election season, commit to listening first, making space for God to work through each conversation, and ensuring that our words reflect His love and wisdom.

Prayer:
Lord, give me ears to truly listen and a heart that seeks understanding before I speak. Forgive me for the times I've spoken out of anger or pride. Help me to be slow to speak and slow to become angry, especially in discussions where opinions differ. Holy Spirit, fill me with Your wisdom, so that my words build bridges rather than barriers. Teach me to reflect Your grace in every conversation, that I might be a peacemaker and a vessel of unity in the Body of Christ. In Jesus's name, amen.

Day 14 | Humility in Disagreements

Do nothing out of selfish ambition or vain conceit. Rather, in humility value others above yourselves, not looking to your own interests but each of you to the interests of the others.
Philippians 2:3-4 (NIV)

Politics can bring out the worst in us when we focus solely on winning arguments or proving our points. But in the kingdom of God, the way of the cross is the way of humility. Paul exhorts us to value others above ourselves, seeking their good, even in disagreements. This is particularly challenging in an election year, where lines are often drawn sharply. However, humility allows us to lay down our pride and listen deeply, respecting the humanity and faith of others. It's not about diminishing your own convictions, but about recognizing that the person you're engaging with is equally beloved by God. When we practice humility, we can engage in political conversations in a way that fosters understanding, respect, and, ultimately, unity.

Prayer:
Jesus, You humbled Yourself for me, becoming obedient to death on a cross. Teach me to walk in that same humility, valuing others above myself, even when we disagree. Help me to let go of selfish ambition and pride, and instead, seek the good of others. In political discussions, help me to see my brothers and sisters through Your eyes, and give me the grace to honor their perspective, even when it differs from mine. May my humility be a reflection of Your heart and a path toward greater unity in Your Body. In Jesus's name, amen.

Day 15 | One Body, Many Parts

Just as a body, though one, has many parts, but all its many parts form one body, so it is with Christ.
1 Corinthians 12:12 (NIV)

The Church is a diverse body, with each member uniquely gifted and called. Our diversity is a strength, not a weakness. However, in the context of political conversations, it can be easy to feel disconnected or even divided from fellow believers who see things differently. Paul's metaphor of the Body of Christ reminds us that while we may have different roles, perspectives, or experiences, we are all part of the same body. Each part is necessary, valuable, and interconnected. Just as a body cannot function properly if one part is cut off, so the Church cannot thrive if we allow divisions to tear us apart. Embrace the diversity of the Body of Christ, recognizing that God has called us to unity, not uniformity. When we honor each other's unique contributions, we reflect the fullness of Christ's love and grace.

Prayer:
Father, thank You for the beautiful diversity within the Body of Christ. Help me to see my brothers and sisters as essential parts of Your Church, each uniquely gifted and called by You. In the midst of political differences, remind me that we are one body, united by Your Spirit. Give me the grace to honor and appreciate the diversity of perspectives within the Church, how your truth is our common ground, recognizing that our unity is found in You. Teach me to value each part of the Body, knowing that together we reflect the fullness of who You are. In Jesus's name, amen.

Day 16 | Choosing Love Over Fear

There is no fear in love. But perfect love drives out fear, because fear has to do with punishment. The one who fears is not made perfect in love.
1 John 4:18 (NIV)

Fear is a powerful force in politics. It can drive people to make decisions based on anxiety, distrust, or the desire for control. But as believers, we are called to operate from a place of love, not fear. Perfect love drives out fear because love trusts in God's sovereignty and goodness. When political rhetoric stirs up fear, we must remember that our ultimate hope is in Christ, not in any earthly leader or system. Love invites us to engage with others—not from a place of suspicion or anxiety, but with open hearts and minds, trusting that God is in control. When we choose love over fear, we can engage in political conversations with peace and compassion, knowing that God's perfect love casts out all fear.

Prayer:
Lord, I confess that fear sometimes creeps into my heart, especially in uncertain political times. Help me to rest in Your perfect love, knowing that You are in control. Let Your love drive out any fear or anxiety I may feel, and replace it with trust in Your plan and purpose. Teach me to engage with others from a place of love, not fear, knowing that Your love is greater than any political agenda. May my words and actions reflect the peace and confidence that comes from being rooted in Your love. In Jesus's name, amen.

Day 17 | Let No Division Be Among You

I appeal to you, brothers and sisters, in the name of our Lord Jesus Christ, that all of you agree with one another in what you say and that there be no divisions among you, but that you be perfectly united in mind and thought.
1 Corinthians 1:10 (NIV)

Division is one of the enemy's greatest tools to weaken the Body of Christ. Paul's appeal to the Corinthians is just as relevant today as it was in the early church: let there be no divisions among you. Political differences can be a breeding ground for division if we allow them to take precedence over our shared faith in Christ. But we are called to be perfectly united in mind and thought, not because we agree on every issue, but because we are all under the lordship of Jesus. The unity of the Church is a powerful witness to the world. When we stand united, despite our differences, we show the world that the love of Christ transcends all barriers.

Prayer:
Jesus, I long for the unity that You prayed for in Your Church. Forgive me for the times I've allowed political differences to create division between me and my brothers and sisters. Help me to pursue unity, even when it requires humility and sacrifice. Let there be no divisions in Your Body, but instead, let us be perfectly aligned with Your will for our lives, in Your love for us, and in our love for one another. May our unity be a testimony to the world of Your love and grace. In Jesus's name, amen.

Day 18 | Overcoming Evil with Good

Do not be overcome by evil, but overcome evil with good.
Romans 12:21 (NIV)

In politically charged environments, it can feel as though evil is winning when division, anger, and hostility are rampant. But Paul's words remind us that we are not called to fight fire with fire. Instead, we are to overcome evil with good. This means that no matter how heated political debates become, we must respond with kindness, grace, and goodness. It is tempting to retaliate when others act unjustly or speak harshly, but the way of Christ is one of love, even toward our enemies. By choosing good over evil, we reflect the heart of Christ and contribute to the healing and unity of the Body of Christ.

Prayer:
Lord, in a world where evil seems to have the upper hand, help me to be a beacon of Your light. Teach me to overcome evil not with anger or retaliation, but with love, grace, and kindness. Help me to reflect Your heart in every situation, even when it is difficult. Let Your goodness flow through me, that I may be an agent of truth, healing and unity in Your Church and in the world. In Jesus's name, amen.

Day 19 | Our True Citizenship

But our citizenship is in heaven. And we eagerly await a Savior from there, the Lord Jesus Christ.
Philippians 3:20 (NIV)

While we may hold citizenship in earthly nations, our ultimate allegiance is to the kingdom of heaven. This perspective should shape how we engage with political matters. Our loyalty is not in any earthly leader or system but in our Savior, Jesus Christ. As citizens of heaven, we are called to live by the values of the kingdom—truth, love, justice, mercy, and peace. This doesn't mean we disengage from political processes, but it does mean that our actions and attitudes should reflect our heavenly citizenship. In all that we do, let us remember that we are ambassadors of Christ, representing His kingdom on earth.

Prayer:
Father, remind me that my true citizenship is in heaven. Help me to live as an ambassador of Your kingdom, reflecting Your light, love, justice, and mercy in all that I do. As I engage with political issues, keep my eyes fixed on Jesus, knowing that my ultimate hope is in Him. Let my life be a testimony of the values of Your kingdom, and may I contribute to the unity and healing of Your Church. In Jesus's name, amen.

Day 20 | *Praying for Our Leaders*

I urge, then, first of all, that petitions, prayers, intercession and thanksgiving be made for all people—for kings and all those in authority, that we may live peaceful and quiet lives in all godliness and holiness.
1 Timothy 2:1-2 (NIV)

Regardless of who is in power, we are called to pray for our leaders. Paul's instruction to Timothy emphasizes the importance of interceding for those in authority, so that we may live peaceful and godly lives. This does not mean that we always agree with our leaders or support every decision they make, but it does mean that we bring them before God in prayer, asking for His wisdom and guidance. When we pray for our leaders, we acknowledge God's sovereignty and trust that He is at work, even in imperfect systems. Let us be faithful in lifting up those in authority, trusting that God's will is being accomplished through our prayers.

Prayer:
Lord, I lift up the leaders of my nation to You today. I pray for wisdom, guidance, and humility for those in positions of authority. Help them to lead with integrity and to make decisions that promote Your will, justice, peace, and godliness. Even when I disagree with their policies, help me to pray for them faithfully, trusting that You are at work. May my prayers contribute to the unity and flourishing of my community and Your Church. In Jesus's name, amen.

Day 21 | The Call to Be Salt and Light

You are the light of the world. A town built on a hill cannot be hidden. Neither do people light a lamp and put it under a bowl. Instead, they put it on its stand, and it gives light to everyone in the house. In the same way, let your light shine before others, that they may see your good deeds and glorify your Father in heaven.
Matthew 5:14-16 (NIV)

Jesus calls us to be both salt and light in the world. As salt, we are to preserve and bring the flavor of Heaven to the world around us, influencing society with the truth and love of God. As light, we are called to shine in the darkness, revealing God's goodness and bringing hope to those who are lost. In the realm of politics, it can be easy to feel overwhelmed by negativity, division, and hopelessness. But Jesus reminds us that we are not to hide our light under a bowl—we are to let it shine brightly so that others may see God through us. This means engaging in political conversations with grace, truth, and love, and being a witness to the character of Christ in every interaction. Let your life be a light that points others to the love and peace of God.

Prayer:
Lord, I thank You for calling me to be salt and light in this world. Help me to live in such a way that others see Your goodness and love through me. In the midst of political division and turmoil, let my words and actions reflect Your truth and grace. Keep my heart soft, my mind clear, and my spirit strong, so that I may shine brightly for You in every conversation and situation. May my life be a testimony of Your transforming power, and may all I do bring glory to Your name. In Jesus's name, amen.

Day 22 | *Guarding Our Hearts*

Above all else, guard your heart, for everything you do flows from it.
Proverbs 4:23 (NIV)

Our hearts are the wellspring of our actions, words, and decisions. In a politically charged environment, it's easy for our hearts to become hardened by frustration, anger, or fear. But Proverbs urges us to guard our hearts diligently, for everything we do flows from them. Guarding your heart means staying connected to God in prayer, soaking in His Word, and allowing His peace to rule in your heart. It means not allowing political division to corrupt your love for others or diminish your hope in God's sovereignty. As you engage with political matters, remember to keep your heart soft and open to God, trusting Him to guide you in every decision and interaction. When our hearts are guarded by the love and truth of God, we can respond to the world around us with grace, wisdom, and peace.

Prayer:
Father, help me to guard my heart in this season. I know that everything I do flows from it, and I want my life to reflect Your love and truth. Protect me from the bitterness, anger, and fear that can so easily creep in during times of political tension. Instead, fill my heart with Your peace, love, and wisdom. Keep me rooted in Your Word and connected to You in prayer, so that I may respond to the world around me in a way that honors You. Let everything I do flow from a heart that is fully surrendered to You. In Jesus's name, amen.

Day 23 | The Power of Prayer

The prayer of a righteous person is powerful and effective.
James 5:16 (NIV)

Prayer is one of the most powerful tools we have as believers. It connects us to the heart of God and allows us to participate in His work on earth. In the political realm, it's easy to feel powerless in the face of large-scale decisions and events. But Scripture reminds us that the prayers of a righteous person are both powerful and effective. When we pray for our leaders, our communities, and our nation, we are actively engaging in the work of God. Prayer can change hearts, heal divisions, and bring about transformation in ways that no human effort can. As you pray for this election season, remember that your prayers are not in vain. God hears them and is at work, even when we cannot see it. Trust in the power of prayer to bring about God's will in every situation.

Prayer:
Lord, thank You for the gift of prayer and the power it holds. I come before You today, lifting up my community, my nation, and its leaders to You. I ask for Your wisdom, guidance, and peace to prevail in this election season. I trust that You are at work, even when I don't see the immediate results. Help me to remain faithful in prayer, knowing that it is powerful and effective. May Your will be done on earth as it is in heaven. In Jesus's name, amen.

Day 24 | Trusting in God's Sovereignty

I make known the end from the beginning, from ancient times, what is still to come. I say, 'My purpose will stand, and I will do all that I please.
Isaiah 46:10 (NIV)

In times of political uncertainty, it's easy to feel anxious or powerless. But Isaiah reminds us of God's sovereignty—He knows the end from the beginning, and His purposes will stand. No matter what happens in an election, we can rest in the assurance that God is in control. His plans are never thwarted by human actions, and He works all things for the good of those who love Him. Trusting in God's sovereignty allows us to engage with the political process without fear or anxiety, knowing that His kingdom is unshakeable. As you cast your vote, remember that God's will is always being accomplished, even when it seems like things are out of control. Let this truth give you peace, confidence, and hope in the midst of uncertainty.

Prayer:
Father, I trust in Your sovereignty and Your perfect plan. Thank You for the assurance that Your purpose will stand, no matter what happens in the world around me. Help me to rest in the knowledge that You are in control and that nothing is outside of Your reach. As I engage with the political process, give me peace and confidence, knowing that Your kingdom is unshakeable. Let my hope always be in You, and not in the systems or leaders of this world. In Jesus's name, amen.

Day 25 | Kingdom Minded

Your kingdom come, Your will be done, on earth as it is in heaven.
Matthew 6:10 (NIV)

As citizens of heaven, our primary focus is on the kingdom of God, always aware that we serve at the pleasure of our King Jesus. Jesus taught us to pray for His kingdom to come and His will to be done on earth as it is in heaven. This prayer reminds us that our ultimate allegiance is not to any political party or system, but to the rule and reign of Christ. In this election season, it's easy to get caught up in earthly concerns, but we are called to have a kingdom mindset. This means seeking God's will above all else and working to bring His truth, justice, love, and peace into every aspect of our lives. It also means trusting that His kingdom will ultimately prevail, no matter what happens in the political realm. Cast your vote, but let your heart and mind be focused on the eternal kingdom, knowing that God's will is being done on earth, even now.

Prayer:
Lord, I pray for Your kingdom to come and Your will to be done on earth as it is in heaven. Help me to live with a kingdom mindset, seeking Your will above all else. Let my actions and decisions reflect my allegiance to You and Your kingdom. In the midst of political uncertainty, and as I perform my civic duties, please Holy Spirit remind me that Jesus's kingdom is eternal and unshakeable. Give me the grace to trust in Your plan Jesus and to work toward bringing Your truth, love, justice, and peace into every situation. In Jesus's name, amen.

Day 26 | Loving Our Enemies

But I tell you, love your enemies and pray for those who persecute you.
Matthew 5:44 (NIV)

Jesus's command to love our enemies is one of the most challenging teachings in the Bible. It goes against our natural instincts to retaliate or harbor resentment. In the political arena, it can feel especially difficult to love those we perceive as enemies—those whose views oppose our own or who seem to work against what we believe is right. Yet, Jesus calls us to a higher standard. He asks us not only to love our enemies but also to pray for them. This love is not based on agreement or shared values but on the love of Christ, who died for us while we were still sinners. As you navigate political differences, remember that every person is made in the image of God and is deserving of love and prayer.

Prayer:
Jesus, You have called me to love my enemies and to pray for those who oppose me. This is not easy, but I know that it is Your will. Help me to see others as You see them—as beloved children of God, made in Your image. Soften my heart toward those I disagree with, and give me the grace to love and pray for them. Let Your love flow through me, overcoming any bitterness, anger, or division. May my life be a reflection of Your love, even in the most challenging situations. In Your name, amen.

Day 27 | Unity in Diversity

> *There is neither Jew nor Gentile, neither slave nor free, nor is there male and female, for you are all one in Christ Jesus.*
> *Galatians 3:28 (NIV)*

The Body of Christ is beautifully diverse, made up of people from every tribe, tongue, and nation. Yet, in Christ, we are all one. Holding up the banner of grace and truth. This unity in diversity is a powerful testimony to the world of God's love and grace, built on a foundation of His holiness. Political differences may exist within the Church, but our shared identity in Christ is far more important than any earthly distinction. We are united by the blood of Jesus, not by our political affiliations or cultural backgrounds. As you engage with believers who may think differently than you, remember that you are part of the same Body—one in Christ Jesus. Let this truth guide your interactions, allowing you to celebrate diversity while pursuing unity in the Holy Spirit.

Prayer:
Father, thank You for the diversity within the Body of Christ. I celebrate the differences that exist among Your people, knowing that we are all one in Christ Jesus. Help me to remember that my identity is first and foremost in You, not in any earthly label or affiliation. Teach me to value and honor the diversity of perspectives within the Church, even when we disagree. Let Your Spirit of unity dwell richly among us, that we may be a powerful witness to the world of Your love and grace. In Jesus's name, amen.

Day 28 | A Heart of Compassion

Therefore, as God's chosen people, holy and dearly loved, clothe yourselves with compassion, kindness, humility, gentleness, and patience.
Colossians 3:12 (NIV)

Compassion is at the heart of the gospel. Jesus modeled a life of compassion, caring for the poor, healing the sick, and extending grace to the vulnerable and underserved. As His followers, we are called to clothe ourselves with compassion, kindness, humility, gentleness, and patience. In the political realm, it can be easy to lose sight of compassion, especially when emotions run high. But we must remember that every person is deeply loved by God and deserving of compassion, even those we disagree with. Let compassion guide your words and actions, allowing you to respond to others with grace and love. In doing so, you reflect the heart of our King, the Lord Jesus Christ, to a world in need of His love.

Prayer:
Jesus, You have shown me what true compassion looks like. Help me to clothe myself with compassion, kindness, humility, gentleness, and patience in all my interactions. Give me a heart that breaks for the things that break Yours, and the wisdom to respond with love and grace, especially in difficult conversations. Let Your compassion flow through me, so that others may see You in my words and actions. In Jesus's name, amen.

Day 29 | The Fruit of the Spirit

But the fruit of the Spirit is love, joy, peace, forbearance, kindness, goodness, faithfulness, gentleness and self-control. Against such things there is no law.
Galatians 5:22-23 (NIV)

The fruit of the Spirit is evidence of God's work in our lives. As we walk with the Spirit, these qualities—love, joy, peace, patience, kindness, goodness, faithfulness, gentleness, and self-control—should be evident in our words, actions, and attitudes. In the political realm, these fruits are especially important. When we engage in discussions or debates, the way we conduct ourselves matters. Are we displaying love and kindness? Are we promoting peace and exercising self-control? The fruit of the Spirit is a powerful witness to the world of God's transforming power. As you navigate this election season, ask the Holy Spirit to produce these fruits in your life, so that you may reflect the character of Christ in all you do.

Prayer:
Holy Spirit, I ask You to fill me with Your presence and to produce the fruit of the Spirit in my life. Let love, joy, peace, patience, kindness, goodness, faithfulness, gentleness, and self-control be evident in all that I do. Help me to engage with others in a way that reflects Your character, especially in political conversations. Teach me to rely on Your strength, so that I may walk in the Spirit and bear fruit that brings glory to Your name. In Jesus's name, amen.

Day 30 | Keeping the Faith

I have fought the good fight, I have finished the race, I have kept the faith.
2 Timothy 4:7 (NIV)

As this devotional draws to a close, we are reminded that the Christian life is a race of endurance. Keeping the faith means staying true to our calling, even when the road is difficult. In the context of political division and uncertainty, we are called to persevere in love, unity, and faithfulness to Christ. We may not always see immediate results or feel like our efforts make a difference, but God calls us to remain steadfast. As we finish this race, let us keep our eyes on Jesus, the author and finisher of our faith. He is our ultimate hope and victory, and in Him, we will find the strength to persevere until the end.

Prayer:
Lord, thank You for the strength and grace to run this race of faith. Help me to persevere in love, unity, and faithfulness to You, even in the midst of challenges and uncertainty. As I finish this season, I commit to keeping my eyes on You, knowing that You are my ultimate hope and victory. Strengthen me to finish the race well and to keep the faith, always trusting in Your goodness and sovereignty. In Jesus's name, amen.

CONCLUSION

As you've journeyed through these 30 days, remember that our unity in Christ is far more important than any political division. Your vote matters, but how you love, serve, and unite with your brothers and sisters in Christ matters even more. Let this season be marked by a renewed commitment to truth, love, peace, and unity in the Body of Christ, knowing that God's Kingdom is eternal and unshakeable.

www.ingramcontent.com/pod-product-compliance
Lightning Source LLC
Chambersburg PA
CBHW060428050426
42449CB00009B/2185